WANTED

MYSTERY INVESTIGATORS

Are you looking for adventure? Are you curious? Do you like solving challenges — and, most of all, do you want to get your teeth into some of the creepiest, freakiest Great Mysteries of the World?

YOU	**RICHARD**	
Adventurous?	☐	Adventurous? (Adventure is fine as long as there are no big spiders . . . eek!)
Like a challenge?	☐	Like a challenge? (There's nothing I like better than really challenging challenges!)
Curious?	☐	Curious? (Oh yes! Some might say 'nosy'.)

If you can tick all the boxes, join me on a global journey to investigate the unexplained, the bizarre and the downright weird. From monster hunters and terrible yetis, to real-life vampires and werewolf kings, you'll be stunned at some of the strange and spooky things in the world . . .

All these mysteries have baffled the experts and left investigators clueless. My mission is to find out the truth. And I need your help.

Together, we'll weigh up the evidence, look at all the explanations — then you decide which is the best solution. You can even keep track of your solved mysteries by turning to page 103 and recording your verdict!

A word of warning: If you're the nervous type, put this book down now. Some of the mysteries we'll be investigating are pretty scary. The kind of things that might make a person a bit, well, jumpy . . .

What was that?

Did you hear something?

OK, I'd better calm down . . . and breathe . . .

Let's go. Time to explore the world's greatest mysteries!

Richard Hammond

RICHARD HAMMOND'S

GREAT MYSTERIES OF THE WORLD

CREEPY CREATURES

RED FOX

RICHARD HAMMOND'S GREAT MYSTERIES OF THE WORLD: CREEPY CREATURES
A RED FOX BOOK 978 1 849 41713 6

Published in Great Britain by Red Fox,
an imprint of Random House Children's Publishers UK
A Random House Group Company
1 3 5 7 9 10 8 6 4 2

Bind-up edition published by The Bodley Head 2013
This Red Fox edition published 2014

The Random House Group Limited supports the Forest Stewardship Council® (FSC®),
the leading international forest-certification organisation. Our books carrying the FSC label
are printed on FSC®-certified paper. FSC is the only forest-certification scheme supported
by the leading environmental organisations, including Greenpeace. Our paper procurement
policy can be found at www.randomhouse.co.uk/environment

Set in Baskerville Classico 12/17.5pt

RANDOM HOUSE CHILDREN'S PUBLISHERS UK
61–63 Uxbridge Road, London W5 5SA

www.**randomhousechildrens**.co.uk
www.**totallyrandombooks**.co.uk
www.**randomhouse**.co.uk

Addresses for companies within The Random House Group Limited can be found at:
www.randomhouse.co.uk/offices.htm

THE RANDOM HOUSE GROUP Limited Reg. No. 954009

A CIP catalogue record for this book is available from the British Library.

Printed and bound in Great Britain by
CPI Group (UK) Ltd, Croydon, CR0 4YY

CREEPY CREATURES

With special thanks to Amanda Li

CONTENTS

1. The Loch Ness Monster   1

2. The Yeti   29

3. Vampires   57

4. Werewolves   83

    Want to Know More?   101

    Decision Time   103

MYSTERY 1

The
Loch Ness Monster

THE MISSION ...

This is a big one, so hold onto your hunting hats ...
... to find out what – if anything – lives in the murky depths
of Loch Ness.

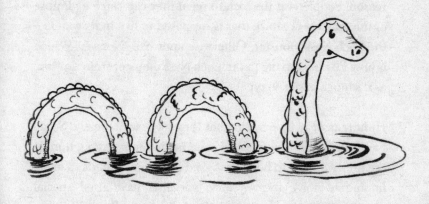

BURNING QUESTIONS

🔥 Is there a monster in Loch Ness?

🔥 If so, why has it never been found?

🔥 Do other lake monsters exist?

MISSION DETAILS

Loch Ness is the most well-known loch in Scotland. A loch, by the way, is the Scottish name for a lake. And there are a lot of lochs in Scotland.

Every year tourists flock to Loch Ness in their thousands, and it is famous all over the world. Is this because the loch is stunningly beautiful? Well – it is – but there's an even bigger reason. People visit the loch to see if they can catch a glimpse of the massive creature that is supposed to live in its waters – the Loch Ness monster. Otherwise known as 'Nessie'. (Which is how I'll be referring to the Loch Ness monster from now on, as it's much easier to type).

Hundreds of people swear that they have seen Nessie. Some have taken photographs and even made films – though most are pretty blurry, to be honest. And it's not just holidaymakers hoping to solve the mystery: scientists have used special scanning equipment to search the dark waters. But still no one has found the monster.

And it seems that Nessie is not the only creature of its kind. There are many more strange and wonderful creatures thought to be living in deep lakes all around the world.

Could these creatures have survived for years without ever being discovered? Read on . . .

THE LOCATION

You can find Loch Ness in the mountainous north of Scotland, in a region called the Highlands.

If you ever visit, you'll see that Loch Ness is no ordinary lake – it's huge!

- 37 kilometres long and extremely deep, a whopping 230 metres at its deepest point. Compare that to the height of the London Eye, a mere 135 metres tall . . .
- The loch is the largest body of fresh water in the whole of Britain – there is more water here than in all the lakes of England and Wales combined

The incredibly large Loch Ness

No wonder it's been so hard to find the Loch Ness monster . . .
This is NOT like looking for the soap in the bath.

Hidden Monsters

Did you know that Nessie is the most famous cryptid
in the world?

(It's OK – I didn't either!) Let me explain.

The word 'cryptid' means 'hidden creature'. (It comes
from the Greek word kryptos which means – no points for
guessing – 'hidden'!)

People who study the Loch Ness monster – as well as other creatures whose existence hasn't been proved – are called 'cryptozoologists'. A pretty long name for a person who's interested in things that might – or might not – exist. (A bit like you and me, really. Hey, we're cryptozoologists! Do we get a badge?)

All the creatures you'll read about in this book would be fascinating to a cryptozoologist. But you can't do a GCSE in this subject, as it is not seen as a 'proper' science. Maybe someone needs to prove Nessie exists for cryptozoology to be taken seriously? Then we'd get a badge...

THE EVIDENCE

There's no shortage of tales about a mysterious creature living in Loch Ness. Some of these go back many, many years.

Strange Stories

Locals once told of the kelpie – a magical and malevolent water monster, also known as a water horse. On land it could apparently turn itself into a real horse. But if someone rode it, it would gallop straight into the loch and the unsuspecting rider would meet a watery death. Was this story a way of warning local children to stay away from the dangerously deep water – or was there any truth behind it?

Spooky Sightings

The earliest sighting of the Loch Ness monster happened way back in the sixth century. The story goes that a monk called St Columba came across a group of men burying a mauled and mangled body. They told the monk that the man had been attacked and killed by a horrible creature in the loch. St Columba ordered one of his (terrified) followers to swim across the loch and fetch the dead man's boat. But the monster was lying in wait for its next victim and it rose to the surface with a terrible roar, its mouth open wide. St Columba raised his hand and made the sign of the cross, exclaiming, 'Stop! Go no further nor touch the man!' The saint was so scary that the monster fled! Maybe he wore a terrifyingly huge hat or something.

St Columba stands up to the Loch Ness Monster. The big bully! (The monster, I mean. And note: no hat. Must've had a REALLY loud voice.)

A Monster Year

Sightings of the monster increased dramatically during one particular year – 1933. A husband and wife, Mr and Mrs McKay, were driving along a new road next to the loch when they noticed a strange disturbance in the dark waters. Going for a closer look, they were amazed (and just a little freaked out) to see a huge creature rolling around in the middle of the loch, creating quite a splash.

Later that year, the creature was spotted again. Another couple driving along by the loch apparently saw 'a most extraordinary form of animal' crossing the road in front of their car. They described the creature as being about 12–15 metres, with a long thin neck like an elephant's trunk. The driver, a Mr Spicer, said, 'I am certain that this creature was of a prehistoric species.' Whatever it was, it soon disappeared, lumbering back into the loch. His comment was interesting though – as some think that Nessie may well be a descendant of a prehistoric creature. More on that later.

Back to 1933 – when in November a man called Hugh Gray also spotted a large object splashing around in the loch. Luckily Mr Gray had his camera with him, so managed to take the first ever photograph of the monster. Some people scoffed at it, saying that whatever the blurry shape was, it didn't prove the monster's existence.

Following these sightings, people began talking about the monster. Visitors came to the loch to look out for the creature and the newspapers soon got wind of the news. Monster mania had begun!

There have been hundreds of sightings of Nessie since then – far too many to list here. Many more photographs have been taken too, but quite a few have been proved to be either fakes or mistakes – objects such as logs or boats.

Photos from the Past

Looking at the photographic 'evidence' of Nessie (and the yeti coming up on page 29), some of the older snaps seem to have been taken by a visually challenged zombie with incredibly shaky hands. They are blurry, out of focus and really not up to today's standards. But if you're thinking you could have taken a better shot, the answer is – no, you probably couldn't.

When it comes to photography, we really have got it easy these days. Digital cameras are so small and simple to use compared to some of the clunky equipment that used to be around (just check out the size of this camera to see what I mean!).

In the early twentieth century, things were very different for photographers. Your camera would probably have looked a bit like this:

And worked like this:

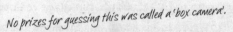
No prizes for guessing this was called a 'box camera'.

The Brownie camera was one of the most popular cameras of its time. And it would have been exactly the kind of gadget a keen monster hunter would have used because it was more portable than all the other cameras around.

But even using a Brownie would be tricky for many of us today.

- To take a shot, you held the Brownie at waist-level and looked down into the finder (see the picture above). Because you had to hold the camera for much longer than today's models, the manual advised you to hold your breath when shooting to make sure the camera stayed still!

- You only had a small number of shots too. Vintage cameras needed to be loaded up with film, so you would usually get 12 or 24 shots. Once you'd used up your film, that was it. And if you accidentally took a pic of your hand, you were stuck with it – no deleting

- Producing a simple photo took much, much longer. The film had to be wound onto a reel before it could be taken out of the camera and put in an envelope. Then on to a dark room for developing. Any exposure to light would destroy all your precious shots

So, try to imagine being on a monster hunt and spotting the most exciting find of your life. As Nessie swam by, you'd get yourself in position with the camera at your waist and wind the film on with a small handle, before you could push the shutter and take the photo. All this while holding your breath! Add into the mix a fast-moving object and all the technical problems of shooting on moving water (the sunlight bounces off it and makes your subject very dark), and it's really a wonder people in the past managed to get any decent photos at all.

Modern-day monster hunters can use cameras with really fast shutter speeds to capture objects moving quickly. Vibration Reduction (VR) helps get rid of any 'shake' – and polarizing filters reduce reflections on the surface of the water. We have the technology – now all we need to do is find the monsters ...

It's a Hoax!
Monster Footprints . . . ?

Following the sightings of 1933, the *Daily Mail* newspaper decided to send a team of professionals to Loch Ness. The team was led by a man called Marmaduke Wetherall, a well-known game hunter whose expert tracking skills had helped him hunt down all kinds of creatures in far-off places, like Africa. But he'd never tried to find anything as big as this before.

Marmaduke dreams of photographing a monster – but with the largest camera in the world and a monkey for an assistant, will he succeed? Wise choice of assistant, though – he works for peanuts.

There was great excitement when Marmaduke actually found the monster's footprints! Plaster casts were taken and sent for scientific assessment. But they turned out NOT to be prints from a mysterious lake monster – they had been made by a stuffed hippopotamus foot, probably the base of an old-fashioned umbrella stand or lampshade. (Yes, readers – sadly, in those days, people thought nothing of shooting a hippo or an elephant and making its limbs into a household accessory.) Cue red faces all round!

Photographic Evidence . . . ?

Probably the most famous photo of Nessie was taken in 1934 by a surgeon called Robert Kenneth Wilson. He and a friend had stopped for a driving break when, suddenly, a sinister shape broke through the surface of the loch. Wilson ran to get his camera and took this picture, which clearly shows the neck of the monster emerging from the water. The surgeon's photograph became a global sensation! For 60 years it was the proof needed of the monster's existence. But, yet again, things were not as they seemed . . .

© KEYSTONE/GETTY IMAGES

The world-famous 'Surgeon's Photo'. People wondered if it had been 'doctored'!

In 1994 the 93-year-old stepson of Marmaduke Wetherall (yes, the very same Marmaduke who had been fooled by those footprints years ago) admitted that the photograph was a fake. He had made the monster in the surgeon's photograph – by sticking a cut-out wooden neck onto a toy submarine! It was, apparently, in revenge for his stepfather being made a laughing stock all those years ago.

Incidents like these show us why trying to find the truth about Nessie is so difficult. Quite a few stories and photos over the years have been made up. Why do people pretend to have seen the monster? Sometimes to make money out of selling their story, sometimes to get attention, and sometimes – just because they can!

The 'monster' was nothing more than a toy and a piece of wood – would you have been taken in by it?

Nessie – the Movie

The most famous piece of film showing what seems to be a creature in the loch was taken in 1960 by monster hunter, Tim Dinsdale. It shows a mysterious hump-like shape crossing the water at high speed and changing direction several times. In 1962 the film was shown on television and was examined by experts. No one has yet proved that it is a hoax. But some believe that Dinsdale was mistaken and all he filmed was a boat.

Whatever was swimming in the loch that day, Dinsdale's film made everyone get more serious about searching for the monster. Brainy students from Oxford and Cambridge universities did the first proper scientific investigation in the summer of 1960, using boats, cameras and echo-sounding equipment. The data they got back was unclear but showed that there may have been 'something' under the water.

In 1962 the grand-sounding 'Loch Ness Phenomena Investigation Bureau' was launched, an organization determined to get to the bottom of the mystery. One of its members was Sir Peter Scott, the grandson of the famous explorer Captain Scott.

The bureau organized volunteers to watch the loch with cameras but, though sightings were made, nothing definite was found. Later, they went underwater and used mini-submarines, sonar technology, and even old-fashioned baiting to investigate the murky waters. (Not sure what they dangled in the depths to attract the monster – a very big fish, perhaps?)

Something was detected moving up and down, possibly diving to the bottom of the loch. Whatever it was seemed to be about six metres in length.

Fast forward to the early 1970s, when a man called Robert Rines decided to set up another array of equipment (the most sophisticated stuff around at the time, including underwater cameras and sonar scanners) to try and find Nessie. In 1975 four of his photographs were made public and there was huge excitement around the world. The photos showed what appeared to be a long-necked creature swimming underwater – they even showed a flipper! This was probably the most exciting discovery yet made.

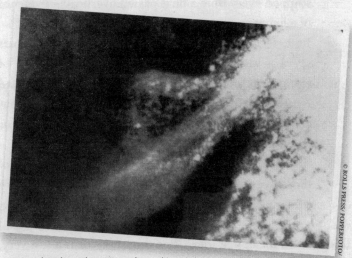

Was this photo the evidence the world needed?

Sir Peter Scott, who was also a skilled artist, painted a picture of two imaginary Nessies coasting along the loch, based on Rines's photographs (see one of them on page 15). Scott was clearly convinced by the photos – but the scientists were less sure. Those who examined them thought they were definitely authentic photos – but that they still did not prove the existence of the monster.

Following the flipper frenzy, several more 'monster missions' were organized. It was clear that many people were convinced enough to spend their time and money trying to find Nessie.

Other expedition findings:

- One search heard strange noises being made by something deep at the bottom of the lake. The noises stopped every time a boat passed overhead – evidence of a living creature?
- In 1987 Operation Deepscan was launched: 24 boats spent a week on the loch using £1million worth of equipment to scan the lake. They thought that they had found something 'larger than a fish' in the waters but could not identify it. Could it have been a monster – or was it perhaps a seal?
- In 2003 the BBC carried out the most extensive search of the loch ever made, using 600 sonar beams and the very latest satellite navigation technology. They found nothing

Does all this mean that there is no monster – or is it just very, very good at hiding from investigators?

Nessie Features

Let's try and get a clearer idea of what the Loch Ness monster could actually look like.

According to eyewitness accounts and photographs, Nessie could have:

- A long snake-like neck
- A longish tail
- Flippers – maybe two, maybe four
- A hump – which could be part of its body, protruding above the surface of the water; some descriptions say the creature has two or more humps

The most popular image of Nessie – the one you'll find on T-shirts and souvenirs – is of a creature with humps. Like this:

One hump or two?

Could Nessie have humps *and* flippers? Is the monster like a giant snake or more like a dinosaur? More coming up . . .

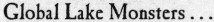

Global Lake Monsters . . .

Nessie isn't the only creature thought to be lurking in the deep. Here are just a few other mystery monsters from around the globe . . .

🌐 The cute and cuddly one . . .

Is there a monster lurking in the depths of Lake Ikeda, Japan? Like Nessie, the creature has a nickname – 'Issie'. There are other similarities too. No one has yet taken a decent picture of the Japanese monster.

🌐 The horrible humpy one . . .

Lake Okanagan in British Columbia is said to be the home of an aggressive monster called Ogopogo. It is described as having a snake-like body and humps – sound familiar? The native Okanakane Indians definitely believe in the monster – they protect themselves by throwing meat for Ogopogo into the lake whenever they cross it!

🌐 The weird whiskery one . . .

A weird-looking 'worm monster' is said to live in Iceland's Lake Lagarfljot. It has been described as a pale, humped animal, about fifteen metres in length, with a long neck and, bizarrely, whiskers! The most recent sighting was in 2012.

MY MISSION

So, what's the best way to find a super-shy monster in a very large lake? Most visitors just watch and wait, hoping that if they hang out at the loch for long enough, Nessie might make a surprise appearance. Almost all leave disappointed.

Professional teams of 'monster hunters' are another thing altogether. These guys have got all the equipment – the scanners, the radars, the latest technology and gadgets. Over the years, many scientific research expeditions have scoured the loch in the hope of finally getting proof of the monster – but most have also come away disappointed . . .

As for me, I'll be driving up to the Highlands and camping out by the loch for a few nights. During the day I'll be observing the loch and sailing out in a small boat – with a few gadgets, of course:

KIT LIST

- 🌀 HIGH-POWERED HUNTING BINOCULARS – to survey the loch and watch out for any mysterious ripples or splashes; fully sealed with a nitrogen gas filling – and waterproof too
- 🌀 A TOP-OF-THE-RANGE CAMERA WITH OPTICAL ZOOM LENS – for long-distance shots
- 🌀 A VIDEO CAMERA WITH NIGHT-TIME INFRA-RED – in case Nessie pops up in the dark

- AN OUTBOARD MOTORBOAT – small and speedy to whizz around all parts of the loch
- A SONAR SCANNER, ECHO-SOUNDERS & HYDROPHONE – on board I'll have a sonar scanner, echo-sounders and I'll be using a hydrophone – an underwater mike (these gadgets will help detect anything large moving through the water, while the microphone should pick up any underwater 'Nessie noises')

MISSION COMPLETED

It has to be said, this monster-hunting business is really quite boring. They should really call it 'monster waiting'. You need a lot of patience – and a lot of snacks – to keep going through the long days and nights of watching and waiting.

I've been camping out on the banks of the loch for a week with all my cameras set up, watching the waters with binoculars for any suspicious movements. I haven't spotted the famous humps – but I have seen quite a few mysterious splashes and ripples (plus a lot of tourists on boats).

However, my scanning equipment did come up with some images of large unknown objects – about two or three metres long. They are really dark and blurry, like most of the photos taken in the loch. The problem is that the water here is really murky. I don't know if these images are logs, seals, schools of fish – or maybe Nessie?

WHAT DO YOU THINK?

There are a lot of theories that people have come up with about Nessie, from prehistoric plesiosaurs to overgrown eels! If you're a Nessie believer – and there are many of you out there – take a look at the two possible explanations below and decide which you think fits best.

Nessie Exists

1. Nessie Is a Plesiosaur

Some people believe that Nessie is a prehistoric creature, one that has survived undiscovered in the loch for many thousands of years. If this is true, Nessie could be a plesiosaur, a meat-eating reptile that existed alongside the dinosaurs around *65 million years ago*. Of course, dinosaurs – and plesiosaurs, as far as we know – are extinct. But could Nessie be the exception – a living example of a species that we believed once died out?

Extinct – or Alive?

You see, we've been proved wrong before about a creature that we thought was extinct. In 1938 a fish called a coelacanth (pronounced see-low-canth) was found alive and well swimming around in the waters of the Indian Ocean. This was an absolutely amazing find. Why? This scary-looking fish – which can grow up to 1.5 metres long – was thought to have become extinct 60 million years ago! Some think that the extreme coldness of the deep water in which the fish was found, and the fact that it has few predators, helped it survived all these years. The coelacanth is living proof that a prehistoric creature can be found living in the modern world. So, why not Nessie?

The coelacanth – a living fossil

There are a few problems with the plesiosaur idea, though:

- 🌀 If Nessie has been living in the loch for thousands of years, scientists say there would have to be more than one monster. There would need to be a whole population of plesiosaurs giving birth to new little Nessies. And so far we haven't seen any sign of a big monster family
- 🌀 What would the monsters eat? Scientists don't think there is enough food in the loch to feed a group of large creatures. There are salmon, plankton and various fish, but there would need to be an enormous amount to feed just one plesiosaur, let alone an entire family
- 🌀 Loch Ness wasn't actually formed until the end of the last Ice Age, about 10,000 years ago. So where did the

plesiosaurs live until the time they entered Loch Ness? The whole of this area was covered in thick ice for hundreds of years, so it's hard to see how they could have survived

- Plesiosaurs are thought to be aquatic reptiles, and reptiles are cold-blooded creatures. A reptile couldn't survive in the freezing waters of Loch Ness – it's just too cold. Also, reptiles breathe air – so Nessie would have to surface in order to breathe. Wouldn't the monster have been found by now if it was regularly coming up for air?

2. Nessie Is a Giant Eel

Some people think that Nessie is actually a mammoth, oversized eel. Could those mysterious humps be those of a giant fish writhing around in the water?

However, there are a few 'buts' to this idea:

- If you look at the behaviour of a normal eel, you'll see that they swim with a 'side to side' winding motion, not by making 'humps' arching out of the water
- If Nessie *was* an eel, it would have to be an absolutely massive one. 'Eely' huge! The largest eel that has ever been discovered is a conger eel weighing a whopping 160kg (350lb), found off the shores of Iceland. Conger eels live in the seas of Great Britain and other parts of northern Europe and can grow up to three metres long. However, they are *not* found in Loch Ness because it is a freshwater lake – and conger eels live in salt water. No eel has ever been found that matches up to the alleged size of the hulking Loch Ness monster . . .

Nessie Doesn't Exist

Those who don't believe in the monster point to the fact that we've been searching for many, many years and, still, nothing has ever been found – even with the latest technology. They believe that it's a story that's got out of hand. And that all the sightings, photographs and films are either fakes or mistakes. So have a look at these Nessie 'mistakes' and see what you think.

1. Nessie the Elephant?

This is one of those ideas that sounds so unbelievable, it might even be true. Recently a man called Neil Clark (who is a museum curator of palaeontology and therefore knows what he's talking about) suggested that early sightings of Nessie were not of a monster at all – but of an elephant! Now, you don't often see a group of elephants having a swim in your local lake, but I promise you, there is a logical explanation to all this. Here goes . . .

Years ago, there were no TVs, computers or DVDs to while away the time. People had to make their own entertainment – perhaps playing the piano, having a sing-along or going to see a show. (Fun!) One popular outing was a visit to a travelling circus, where you could see wild animals and human performers doing tricks and stunts (fortunately, this kind of animal show no longer exists).

Circuses would tour the country, visiting towns and villages to entertain the locals and make some money. They often had lots of exotic animals to transport. Those animals needed a wash now and again. And what better spot for a refreshing bathe than the cool waters of Loch Ness – an ideal stop-off point en route to the city of Inverness?

Neil Clark believes that many of those 1930s sightings could have been the upper part of a bathing elephant and its trunk sticking out from the water. It would certainly account for the 1933 descriptions of the monster's neck being like an elephant's trunk!

But how could this explain so many hundreds of monster sightings since the 1930s?

2. Mistaken Identity

Maybe there's nothing weird living in the loch at all. It is simply a case of people mistaking one thing for another. And, just as importantly, people seeing what they *want* to see. For example, people who spot a seal splashing in the distance might really believe they are seeing a monster – because that's why they've come to Loch Ness!

Other things that have been commonly mistaken for Nessie in the past are:

- Boats
- Pieces of wood/dead trees
- Waves
- The wake of a boat
- Deer swimming across the loch

The loch is incredibly misty too – and swirling fog can make you think you see all sorts of strange things. So, do you think people have been spotting monsters that aren't really monsters for all these years?

3. Nessie Is Tree Gas!

Farting trees? Whoever would have thought it?

If you ever visit Loch Ness, you'll see that there are a lot of pine trees growing close to the water. As the pines die, they fall into

the water, and it's possible that the floating logs get mistaken for the monster. But eyewitness accounts often describe seeing an object that is moving along at speed and causing a lot of disturbance in the water. Now dead trees are exactly that – dead! Meaning that they don't usually move around much – or cause disturbances. Come to think of it, even living trees don't swim very fast. So how could a log behave like a moving monster?

Someone came up with the idea that 'tree gas' propels these dead logs along. This is how it works.

- As the pine trunk slowly becomes rotten, it fills up with gas. It is covered with a layer of tree resin (a sticky substance produced by trees) which effectively seals the trunk and stops the gas from coming out
- Eventually the trunk gets so rotten that it suddenly breaks and all that gas shoots out of a gap, causing the log to pop up to the surface and whoosh along like a jet-propelled rocket! Imagine that one of the log's branches is sticking out of the water, just like a monster head, and you've got yourself a super speedy Loch Ness monster!

4. Weird Waves

Could a combination of wind and water create the effect of a swimming monster? There is an unusual event that occurs in some very long, very cold lakes, just like Loch Ness. It is called a *seiche* (pronounced 'saysh'). It's caused by the action of wind on the surface water, which suddenly forces a lot of water to one end of the lake. When the wind stops, the water begins to

27

move back and forth – a bit like the movement of the water when you get out of a bath. All this movement – which can go on for as long as a week – causes strange disturbances in the water that may not look natural. It could even cause a log caught up in the seiche to look as if it is moving around and alive.

Would this phenomenon account for the many Nessie 'sightings'? If it is the reason, this could also very well explain similar 'monsters' found in other large lakes around the globe.

YOU DECIDE

In the end, the only way of proving that the Loch Ness monster exists is to actually catch it – or at least take pictures that show it clearly and unarguably to be a monster.

So where do *you* stand on Nessie? Turn to the back of the book to review your findings.

The Yeti

THE MISSION ...

. . . to find out if a mysterious ape-like creature lives in the mountains of the Himalayas.

BURNING QUESTIONS

- Does the yeti really exist – or is it just a myth?
- If it's real, what kind of creature is it?
- Is the yeti dangerous?

MISSION DETAILS

The soaring mountains of the Himalayas are remote, beautiful – and dangerous. Many have lost their lives here, attempting to climb Everest, the highest mountain in the world.

© ROBERT HARDING PICTURE LIBRARY / SUPERSTOCK

Despite the harsh, freezing conditions, it is said that a huge, hairy creature lives high up among the snow and ice. A creature that is unknown to humankind.

The locals call it the yeti; westerners sometimes call it the 'abominable snowman'.

Whichever name you prefer, the yeti has been the subject of all kinds of investigations, TV documentaries and horror movies.

Those who have seen the beast say it is a hulking hairy figure, about two to three metres tall. With a cone-shaped head and the face of an angry gorilla, it's not the kind of thing you'd want to come across on a dark night (or even a sunny afternoon, for that matter!).

Even scarier is the stinky smell that accompanies the beast. According to eyewitnesses – or should we say *nose*-witnesses – your average yeti is about as whiffy as your dad's trainers filled with warm cheese and left in the sun . . . *pee-ew!*

But, despite many sightings – of the beast itself and also of many huge footprints – still no one has captured an abominable snowman or proved beyond doubt that it really exists. So, when you've seen the evidence, will you be a yeti believer?

THE LOCATION

The Himalayas are a truly spectacular range of mountains in Asia. Incredibly high, they are often called the 'roof of the

world'. And no wonder. They include Mount Everest, the highest peak on Earth, standing at 8,848 metres (29,029 feet)!

The Himalayas are made up of two mountain ranges, separated by a wide valley. The mountains are a mammoth 2,500 kilometres long, spanning parts of northern India, Nepal, Bhutan and Tibet. At the higher parts, thick snow covers the mountains all year round and the temperature rarely rises above freezing point. *Brrr* . . .

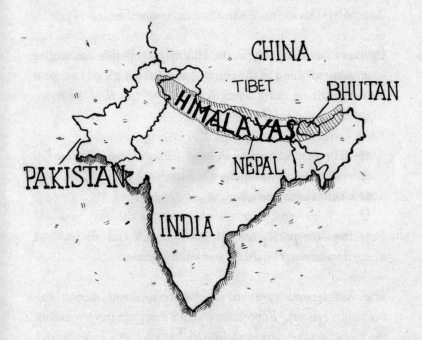

The yeti is supposed to live in the higher regions, where conditions are really extreme. If it exists, it must be an incredibly tough creature to survive in the ice, wind and savage

storms that frequently batter the mountains. But in many ways the Himalayas are the ideal place for a creature that doesn't want to be seen. As it's so inaccessible to humans, it's easy to hide . . .

THE EVIDENCE

The peoples of the Himalayas have told stories about the yeti for centuries. The name itself comes from the Tibetan words *yeh-teh* which mean 'man-bear'. (Though most witnesses say that the yeti looks more like a human crossed with an ape.)

Different cultures living in the Himalayas tell different stories – some are terrified of the yeti and see it as a dark and magical creature. Others don't seem too bothered. Some of the more frightening tales tell of:

- The yeti appearing in local villages to attack and kill yaks (and occasionally a human – see page 40)
- Yetis kidnapping people
- A belief that if you look a yeti in the eye, you will become paralysed with fear, get sick and die (my old headmaster could do something similar)

The yeti legend came to the western world during the twentieth century. Reports of a weird furry creature roaming the mountains began circulating in the late 1800s, but it wasn't until the 1920s that many more sightings began to be reported. This was because western explorers and climbers began to visit this remote area more often.

One of the earliest accounts comes from 1921, when an expedition team to Everest was scaling the north face of the mountain. Looking up, they noticed some mysterious dark figures moving about in the snow, high above them. Who – or what – could be up there?

By the time the mountaineers reached the spot, the figures were gone. All they could find was some large, human-like footprints.

The team leader, Bury, thought they might have been made by a wolf, but the local guides disagreed. They said the prints were from a wild man of the snows – *metoh kangmi*. This was later – and wrongly – translated by a reporter as the abominable snowman. The name stuck, even though the creature looks *nothing* like a snowman. But looking at this illustration – it is 100 per cent abominable!

Definitely hairy – definitely scary!

A few years later, in 1925, a famous incident occurred when a photographer on a British expedition reported seeing a creature near the world's largest glacier, the Zemu. From a distance of around 200 metres, he watched the creature for about a minute, as it wandered around uprooting bushes (presumably for a snack). He said:

'Unquestionably, the figure in outline was exactly like a human being, walking upright . . . It showed up dark against the snow and, as far as I could make out, wore no clothes.'

The creature soon disappeared and the photographer (who hadn't had time to take a picture – *duh*) later found fifteen footprints, similar to human ones, in the snow.

'The marks of five distinct toes and the instep were perfectly clear, but the trace of the heel was indistinct . . .'

Fascinating footprints

The real footprint of the Yeti?

This incredible footprint, and others like it, were found and photographed by British climbers Eric Shipton and Michael Ward in 1951. They formed part of a long trail of prints that eventually disappeared into the ice. The prints had certainly been made by a creature that walked on two feet, like a human. (All creatures that walk on two feet are known as bipeds.)

'What it is, I don't know, but I am quite clear it is no animal known to live in the Himalaya, and that it is big' – Eric Shipton

Each footprint was 33cm wide and 45cm long – much bigger than a normal human foot, as you can see from the photograph. It was also very deep, so whatever made the print was something large and heavy.

Many people believe that these unexplained prints are still the best evidence we have that the yeti exists.

Not Yeti?

Legendary mountaineers Sir Edmund Hillary and Tenzing Norgay broke all records when they made the very first ascent of Mount Everest in 1953. There was huge excitement all over the world. And more excitement still when the pair found mysterious footprints on the way up . . .

Hillary became fascinated by the yeti stories and returned to the Himalayas in 1960 on a quest to find the abominable snowman. He was shown a 350-year-old cone-shaped scalp at a remote monastery which was said to be that of a yeti. The scalp was brought back to England for closer inspection. Was this the evidence needed to prove its existence? Sadly, the scalp was examined and thought to be a fake made from the skin of a Himalayan goat. (Not everyone agrees with this, though – some still believe it could be a yeti's head.)

Sir Edmund Hillary puzzles over the scalp

© POPPERFOTO/GETTY IMAGES

Hillary also brought back some small samples of fur, but these were later found to be from the rare Tibetan blue bear, which lives in the Himalayas.

Anyway, after all his investigations, Hillary eventually decided that the yeti was mythical and that the footprints he had seen on his ascent of Everest were probably human ones that had been melted by the sun.

The Hunt Goes On ...

One of the biggest searches in yeti history happened in 1954 when a research team was sent to the Himalayas by the *Daily Mail* newspaper. A huge number of footprints were discovered, followed and photographed. Some were found to be human – but others were larger and could not be identified.

Sightings and hearings have continued over the years. In 1970 Don Whillans, a British climber on Mount Annapurna, heard strange and eerie cries in the distance, like nothing he'd ever heard before. His Sherpa guide immediately identified it as the call of a yeti. Later that night, Whillans saw a dark, ape-like figure moving around near their camp. Bet he didn't sleep very well ...

The next day, Whillans's sighting was proved true when large deep footprints were found in the snow. But the most exciting part came later that day. Whillans was in his tent when the dark creature returned. He watched the strange figure through binoculars for about 20 minutes as it rooted around for food and pulled branches from a tree, before running off. To this day, he remains convinced that the animal was neither a human nor an ape ...

Secrets of the Shrivelled Hand

Why would anyone keep a crusty, brown, shrivelled-up old hand for years? Perhaps they thought it might come in 'handy' one day?!

Well, the monks of the remote monastery of Pangboche in the Himalayas kept a hand just like this. They believed that it was the hand of a yeti, and that it would protect them from bad luck.

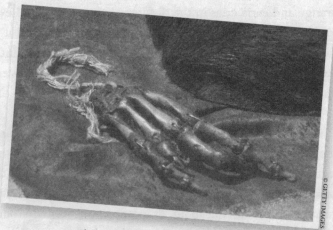

The hand, all shrivelled and brown. Eeew!

In 1958 an explorer called Peter Byrne was shown the hand while on an expedition to search for the abominable snowman. Naturally, he was keen to find out if it really did belong to the famed yeti. But it would need a proper scientific analysis and it would need to be taken to a lab.

The monks didn't want to let the hand out of their sight. But, on a second visit, Byrne managed to persuade them to let him have just one of the fingers in return for a sum of money. (The remainder of it was later stolen from the monastery – clearly a very popular hand!)

The finger was 9cm long, 2cm at the widest part, curled and black at the end with an extended nail. The hand itself was said to be about the size of a human's.

The 'yeti's finger' was smuggled out of the country into the UK, but what happened after that is a mystery. Many years passed. In 2008 the finger was finally found nestling in the vaults at the Royal College of Surgeons in London. Not such a strange thing when you consider some of the other items here. Its most famous collection – the Hunterian Collection – includes:

- pickled organs from soldiers who fought in the Battle of Waterloo
- Winston Churchill's false teeth
- the skeleton of Charles Byrne, the 2.31m tall 'Irish giant'!

In 2011 DNA from the finger was analysed – and it was found to be 'of human origin'. So, if the finger is from a yeti, then the mysterious beast is even more like a human than anyone thought! But it's more likely to be from a real human – maybe one of the monks donated it?

Yeti Attack!

In 1974 a savage attack took place in the remote Machermo Valley. A young Sherpa woman called Lhakpa Dorma was found wounded and unconscious, while around her lay the bodies of several yaks. They had been killed and half eaten by an unidentified, ferocious creature . . .

When Lhakpa recovered, she described how she had been herding her yaks when she was attacked by a creature she thinks was a yeti. It came up from behind her, grabbing her round the neck and throwing her down some distance away. She then watched in terror as the creature began to attack and kill her yaks. According to her description, the yeti had huge teeth, a wrinkled face, long nails and moved incredibly fast.

All these years on, the old lady is still alive – and still convinced that she had a lucky escape from the yeti. What could have attacked her and her livestock? Was it a bear – or the real abominable snowman?

The Sherpas of the Himalayas

Despite the harsh conditions, thousands of people live in the Himalayas. Of these, the Sherpas are probably the most well-known in the western world. They live high up in the mountains in the north-eastern part of Nepal. Many Sherpa villages are found perched in precarious positions on terrifyingly high ledges and slopes, some as high up as

4,267 metres. There are no roads or cars – hiking is the usual way of getting around. Some Sherpa children climb the equivalent of a skyscraper just to reach school every day! Nobody 'pops to the shops'. It is tough; really, really tough. But great snowball fights . . . if you've got the energy after hiking home from school.

Sherpas are often employed to help trekkers and mountaineers on their expeditions to Everest, as they are used to the high altitude and can usually carry much heavier loads than western visitors.

Sherpas keep herds of yaks – a kind of shaggy-haired ox with horns that is perfectly adapted to living at high altitude. Yaks are incredibly important to the people of the Himalayas – they provide milk, meat and cloth, and are a very useful method of transport.

You looking at me? An unfriendly yak

More Yeti Hunters

In 2008 a team of Japanese yeti hunters photographed footprints, about 20cm long, on snow in the Dhaulagiri mountain range in western Nepal. The expedition leader, Mr Takahashi, believed them to be prints of the yeti.

In fact, Mr Takahashi also believed that he had seen a yeti on a previous expedition in 2003. He described his sighting as follows:

'It was about 200 metres away in silhouette. It was walking on two legs like a human and looked about 150 centimetres tall.'

Reinhold Messner, one of the world's most famous, record-breaking mountaineers, also returned to the Himalayas after he caught sight of a yeti in 1986. He described his yeti as 'big' and 'stinking'! And he was determined to get to the bottom of the mystery.

Messner spent years visiting the Himalayas and talking to the locals about the yeti. He eventually came to the conclusion that the yeti was probably a large brown Tibetan bear, rather than a mysterious unknown ape.

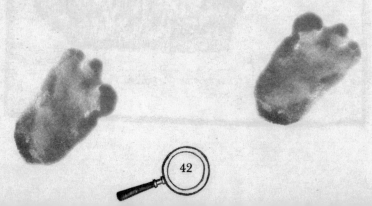

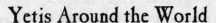

Yetis Around the World

The legend of an ape-man creature does not only appear in the Himalayas. Mystery beasts resembling the yeti have been reported in many other parts of the world. They include:

- The Sasquatch of North America
- The Yowie in Australia
- The Hibagon in Japan
- The Almasty of Russia

and many others . . .

Probably the most famous of these is the Sasquatch – more commonly known as 'Bigfoot' – who is said to roam forests and woods in parts of North America.

There are many similarities between the yeti and Bigfoot. Both are tall, hairy, ape-like creatures that walk on two feet and have long arms and short necks. Both are feared. Both have big feet. Like this:

This is why the creature isn't called Smallfoot. Print found in Bridgewater, Massachusetts, USA.

Bigfoot sightings began to be reported in the 1800s (when large footprints were found near the Rocky Mountains in Canada) and they have continued ever since.

In 1995 a forest patrol officer in the Snoqualamie Forest of Washington heard something moving about and making a splashing noise. He leaned over a ridge to see a hulking ape-like animal staring at him.

One of the most famous pieces of 'evidence' comes from northern California where, in 1967, two men called Roger Patterson and Bob Gimlin actually captured Bigfoot on film. Their footage showed a hairy ape walking across a clearing, then looking around – almost as if he knew he was being watched. Some people think the film is a hoax and that Bigfoot is actually a man dressed up in an ape costume. Others are convinced the film is genuine. No one has proved it either way.

Roger Patterson had a cast made of the footprints left by the creature – they were 37cm long with five toes. Just like the yeti.

Whatever you believe, there's no doubt that Bigfoot is big news in North America.

Identify the Yeti

Just in case you ever come across a yeti, here's what to look out for, according to eyewitness reports:

- It is an extremely fast mover. Not one has been seen standing still
- It walks standing upright, like a human
- It is covered in dark reddish-brown hair
- It makes a weird high-pitched whistling noise
- It is tall and looks like a combination of a man and an ape
- It is very good at avoiding being seen or photographed!

MY MISSION

I'll be travelling to the Nepal region of the Himalayas to see if I can spot the yeti – or at least its footprints. I'll be trekking at high altitude, and camping out at night. It's going to be really, really cold – so I'll need some serious cold weather kit.

KIT LIST

- DOWN JACKET, WOOLLY HAT, SKI GLOVES AND BALACLAVA – to keep me toasty warm
- TREKKING BOOTS WITH EXTRA ICE GRIPPERS ATTACHED – there's a lot of ice and snow up here
- SUNGLASSES AND SUN CREAM – the sun is really strong even though it's cold
- WALKING POLES – to help get a grip on the slippery ground
- MAP AND COMPASS – it would be easy to get lost in these mountains)
- WATER BOTTLE, CAMPING STOVE AND EASY-COOK FOOD SUPPLIES
- HIGH-ALTITUDE TENT, EXTRA-THICK DOWN SLEEPING BAG
- ICE AXE – to help me get across any icy slopes
- LONG-LENS CAMERAS, VIDEO CAMERA AND BINOCULARS

Taking it easy

At very high altitudes (anything above 2,500 metres) the amount of oxygen in the air begins to decrease. And the higher you climb, the lower it gets. This can have a huge impact on

your body. Some people are unlucky and get altitude sickness – which makes you feel sick and dizzy, with headaches and breathlessness.

All trekkers and climbers to high mountains need to take things slowly, spending a couple of days at each level to let their body adjust as they climb higher. This process is called 'acclimatization'.

Everyone reacts differently to high altitudes, but I'm hoping I'm not going to suffer too much. Unfortunately, when venturing above 3,000 metres, 75 per cent of people will experience 'mountain sickness' . . .

The scariest airport in the world

First of all, I have to get to the Himalayas. And I have a feeling that the journey is going to be even worse than bumping into the most ferocious yeti. The first part is easy – simply fly to Kathmandu, the bustling capital city of Nepal. The yeti myth is everywhere in Kathmandu – I could stay at the Yak and Yeti Hotel, then fly up to the mountains on Yeti Airlines!

But next is the bit I am dreading. Why? I will have to get into a tiny twenty-seater aircraft and land at what is supposed to be *the most dangerous airport in the world*. This is the place where most climbers arrive before they attempt Everest. Welcome to Lukla Airport . . .

© BEN PIPE / ROBERT HARDING PICTURE...

It's not even an airport really; more of a tiny – and scarily short – strip of tarmac, only 450 metres long. This 'runway' has been built right on the edge of a steep valley, 2,860 metres up, with a sheer drop on one side. The landing is nerve-racking – very fast and very bumpy – and you often have to descend through dense cloud. Which is never good when you're in a small plane.

MISSION COMPLETED

I made it into (and out of) the world's most dangerous airport. I almost lost the entire contents of my stomach, but not sure if that was due to the bumpy flight or altitude sickness . . .

It was cold, lonely and a bit spooky. I saw a lot of yaks (yak-loads in fact) – but most importantly, I saw these.

Yes, my very own yeti footprints!

They were big – about 40cm long – and deep. The fresh prints went snaking around in a trail into some trees, then disappeared. No funny smells, no weird whistling or anything else. Just footprints. But big ones. Bigger than mine, anyway.

So I'll be adding my bit of evidence to the many others from over the years.

WHAT DO YOU THINK?

Is the yeti a real creature? It's 'make your mind up' time . . .

The Yeti Doesn't Exist

Some think that the 'yeti' is just a regular mountain creature that has been mistaken for something more sinister. It's true that many animals do live in the Himalayas – though very few are found above 550 metres because of the intense cold, snow and ice.

Animals living at high altitudes need to have thick skins and fur to keep warm. Many will hibernate during the winter months, when there isn't much food around, or move down to the lower levels.

Here are a few examples of Himalayan mountain wildlife:

- *The Tibetan blue bear*: incredibly rare and almost never seen; shaggy fur, greyish black, walks on all fours
- *The black bear*: can grow to almost two metres long, but does not generally attack other mammals; lives on ants, grubs, nuts and leaves
- *The brown bear*: heavier and larger than the black bear, it lives in the higher parts of the mountains, eating plants, goats and sheep
- *Snow leopard*: very rare and hardly ever seen, snow leopards have thick spotted fur and prey on deer, birds and tahrs (see below)
- There are also *wolves, martens, foxes, langur monkeys, red pandas* and *Himalayan tahrs* – a cross between a mountain goat and sheep.

It's unlikely that someone could think a goat or a wolf was a yeti – but a bear standing on its hind legs is a possibility. Different types of bears live in forests all over the world too, so this could explain many of the sightings in other countries.

But what about some of the strongest evidence there is for the yeti – the many footprints that have been found? These prints have been studied by experts who've agreed that:

- they are not from an ape or a bear or other forest creature
- they don't come from any animal that we know of

How can they be explained? One suggestion is that the yeti prints are just normal tracks, made by animals or perhaps by local people. But something has happened to them to make them look unusual . . .

A Trick of the Sun?

Imagine an ordinary animal track in the snow with the sun shining down on it. The warmth melts the snow and, depending on the angle of the sun's rays, completely alters the shape of the print. It can become bigger, longer, more dramatic looking – and it could end up appearing like that of some weird, unexplained creature. Could this be the reason for all those mysterious tracks?

Famed mountaineer Reinhold Messner thinks so. And after years of exploring the Himalayas he believes that the 'yeti'

is actually a brown bear, one that sometimes walks upright on its hind legs, as well as on all fours. The bear is known locally as *chemo* and lives at altitudes of 3,500–5,500 metres. Because it is nocturnal, it isn't often seen by humans, so he thinks this has added to the mystery over the years.

But if it is just a bear, where did the idea of the yeti come from? Perhaps the yeti is the 'bogey-man' of the Himalayas – a figure of fear talked about in stories to frighten locals (and make their kids behave!) and to explain away the occasional yak attack.

The Yeti Exists

But if the yeti does exist, what *is* it exactly? There are two schools of thought:

1. It's a Giant Ape
Some believe that the yeti may be a descendant of a prehistoric ape that lived in parts of Asia hundreds of thousands of years ago. This extinct giant ape is called *Gigantopithecus*. Its existence

was only discovered in 1935 when remains of its (incredibly large) teeth were found in China.

Gigantopithecus was supposed to have been the largest ape that ever lived, a kind of real-life King Kong. It is estimated to have been a massive three metres (nearly ten feet) high and to have weighed up to 540 kilograms (1,200lb) – that's two or three times more than a gorilla!

Many scientists believe that this giant ape roamed South-east Asia for nearly a million years before becoming extinct roughly 100,000 years ago. No one knows why it died out.

Or did it? Some yeti enthusiasts believe that the yeti is a direct descendant of *Gigantopithecus*. They think that the species could have survived unknown in the rugged mountains for thousands of years, adapting as time passed by.

However, there is no evidence of this ancient ape anywhere but Asia – so how would this account for sightings of Bigfoot and other similar creatures in other parts of the world? Tricky . . .

2. It's a Man (Sort of . . .)

Some people have another idea. They point to the fact that the yeti looks a bit like a man to say that it might be something human. They think that it could have evolved from Neanderthals – an extinct species of human. Neanderthal humans lived in Europe but disappeared completely about 25,000 years ago. This was 10,000 years after the arrival of

modern humans in Europe (that's us), so for many years, two 'types' of human lived at the same time. No one knows why the Neanderthals died out, but our species lived. One theory is that we were just better equipped for survival.

Is this what Neanderthal man looked like?

The theory is that Neanderthals may have retreated to mountains and forests thousands of years ago and lived completely apart from modern humans. As the years went by, they became wild – and the yeti is the result!

However, very few (if any) scientists think this is possible. One of the problems with this idea is that Neanderthal man used tools – and the yeti has never been seen doing a spot of DIY! Would he/she really have lost this useful skill?

YOU DECIDE

Scientists know for a fact that we haven't discovered all the species of animal in the world, not by a long shot – and there are definitely new creatures out there waiting for us to find and classify them. There are also creatures like the coelacanth (see page 21) which have amazed experts because they were thought to have become extinct millions of years ago. Could the yeti be another creature that defies scientific belief?

Make up your mind! Turn to the back to record your verdict.

THE MISSION...

... to find out if bloodsucking vampires really do exist.

BURNING QUESTIONS

🔥 What is a vampire, exactly?

🔥 How do you know if someone is a vampire?

🔥 How can you get rid of one?

MISSION DETAILS

Think of a vampire – what springs to mind? A fanged man dressed in black lying in a coffin? A pale-faced high-school student who is in love with a human? A flying monster with extraordinary strength and super-senses?

These days, a vampire could be any one of the above. There are even vampires who are vegetarians (they try to avoid blood – but I hear it's fangtastically hard ...).

The vampire myth goes back for centuries, but nowadays vampires are more popular than ever. You can't move for

yet another blockbuster movie, TV series or bestselling book featuring flocks of fanged fiends.

These days vampires are so popular, they even get fang mail! (OK, I promise I'll stop with the 'fang' jokes. Well, I'll try. Sometimes there's not a fang I can do about it ... sorry!)

But what exactly *is* a vampire? He or she is a member of the 'undead'. In other words, the vampire is neither dead nor alive but exists in a kind of limbo between the two states. A vampire exists for ever (unless some brave person manages to destroy it – more on that later) but must drink human blood in order to survive. It does this by catching a human – any human will do as long as he/she has got a decent blood supply – and biting their neck with its sharp fangs. The vampire can then drink the human's blood and feel a whole lot better. The human, however, feels considerably worse. Following the bite, the victim turns into a vampire too.

Fictional vampires are everywhere – but what about in real life? Could there be one living down the road from you? 'Necks' door, perhaps? Oops. That's worse than the fang fing. Sorry!

My mission is to investigate the fictions and realities of the vampire world and find out if the vampire stories have any truth in them . . .

THE LOCATION

Myths and legends about bloodsucking creatures are told all over the world, from Asia and Africa to the Americas. But the best-known vampire story of all comes from Europe – Eastern Europe to be exact. It is the story of Dracula.

The famous Count Dracula of Transylvania

Though Dracula is a fictional character, he was based on a very real person called Vlad the Impaler (the name's a bit of a clue to the horrible things he did). Vlad came from a spooky-sounding place called Transylvania.

Transylvania is a region of a country called Romania. Its name literally means 'beyond the woods', as much of Transylvania was at one time covered in forest. It has been taken over by different countries and empires during its history, including the Roman Empire and the Hungarian Empire. But the name Transylvania will always be associated with haunted castles, dark forests and, of course, vampires . . .

THE EVIDENCE

Tales of the undead have been around from ancient times, in many different cultures. One of the oldest images ever found is on a vase from ancient Persia (founded in the sixth century BC), which shows a man struggling with a creature that is trying to suck its blood. Roman and Greek myths feature horrifying tales of creatures such as the blood-devouring lamia and the striges, an evil bird that feeds on human flesh and blood. In fact, most countries have myths and legends that feature evil spirits or creatures that drink blood.

Vampires as we know them today – dressed in black, blood-red lips and deathly pale white skin: you know the kind of thing – are the type found in Eastern European folklore in the late seventeenth and eighteenth centuries. In Eastern Europe, the threat of vampires was taken very seriously indeed. Transylvanians believed in 'strigoi' (their name for the undead). These ghastly creatures walked the earth because they hadn't been buried properly or had led an evil life. The thought of a vampire being on the loose struck terror into people's hearts. They might have dug a grave to try and find the offending corpse and get rid of it. Driving a stake through *its* heart was one way of doing this (and still the most effective way to wipe out a vampire, according to the experts).

In the 1700s stories of vampires began to circulate in Western Europe too. Bram Stoker, an Irish author who lived in London in the 1800s, researched these legends and was inspired to write his famous horror story – *Dracula*. The most influential book in vampire history was published in 1897 and made Mr Stoker famous all over the world.

© BUYENLARGE/SUPERSTOCK

Bram's bloodthirsty bestseller

The Dreaded Dracula

In the story of *Dracula*, a young English lawyer called Jonathan Harker travels to Transylvania to meet the mysterious Count Dracula on a business matter. Ignoring the bad omens along the way – garbled warnings from terrified villagers, his carriage attacked by wolves (a bit like when those Scooby Doo guys say, 'Let's split up,' and don't

see trouble coming) – Harker finally arrives at Dracula's very large and very spooky castle. He is relieved to find that Dracula is a polite and intelligent gentleman. However, as the days go by, things get nasty. Harker realizes that the count is no gentleman, but an evil vampire who wants to suck his blood and make him a member of his 'undead' gang. Though he is trapped in the castle, Harker manages to escape from Dracula's clutches by climbing the castle walls, and eventually makes it back to the safety of England.

But England isn't safe for long . . . Dracula soon turns up – in a small seaside town called Whitby, in the north-east. He attacks Harker's friend Lucy, who becomes a vampire too. But in true vampire-hunter style, Harker gets his revenge on Dracula when he returns to Transylvania to get rid of the evil vampire once and for all. Hurrah!

Today, in Whitby, there are Dracula mementoes everywhere – there's even a 'Dracula Experience' for tourists where the entire story is re-enacted and you can watch a model of Dracula slowly rising from his coffin!

Dracula is a great story, but it is just that – a story. However, Count Dracula was said to have been inspired by two ghastly real-life characters. The first is:

Very Bad Vlad

'Vlad the Impaler', as Vlad Tepes was known, was born in Transylvania in 1456, though he actually ruled a region called

Wallachia, south of Transylvania. If you'd been unlucky enough to live here in the fifteenth century, you would have done well to avoid Vlad. A ruthless and violent man, he used his power to have thousands of people killed, often by being impaled on long spikes (hence the nickname). No wonder his name struck fear into people's hearts . . .

Like Count Dracula, Vlad lived in a spooky castle, and rumour has it that he drank his victims' blood. He was also known locally as 'Vlad Dracul' because *dracul* means 'devil' in Romanian – which, of course, is where Bram Stoker got the idea for Dracula's name.

Vlad sports a Transylvanian trend – the horizontal moustache

This charming man was killed in 1476 during a battle against the Turks. It is said that his tomb was later found to be empty. People took this as a sign that Vlad was a vampire, who had left his grave to go in search of more blood.

The Blood Countess

Another equally horrible figure was the Countess Elizabeth Bathory, aka the 'Blood Countess'. She came from Eastern Europe too, living in Hungary in the seventeenth century. The countess had a barbaric beauty regime which consisted of killing young girls so she could bathe in, and drink, their blood. For some reason, she thought that this would keep her looking young and beautiful! Fortunately, the Blood Countess was arrested in 1610 and locked up in a tower for the rest of her life. The local girls could now breathe a sigh of relief – phew . . .

The Countess takes time to pose for a portrait – in between blood baths . . .

Modern Day Vampires

You'd find it hard to come across two more unpleasant people than Bad Vlad and the Blood Countess, but were they really vampires – or just very evil people?

There have been many reports of vampire activity since those times, but let's fast forward to the twentieth century, where some very interesting real-life accounts have taken place. Both happen to be in good old London town . . .

The London Vampire

Daytime. A quiet street in London, 1922. Not the most likely location for a vampire attack – but that is exactly what is supposed to have happened. On 16 April 1922 a man was admitted to London's Charing Cross Hospital with a mysterious deep wound in his neck. He had no idea how he had got it. All the man could remember was that he had been walking down Coventry Street (near Piccadilly Circus) on his way to work when he felt an agonizing, stabbing sensation in his neck. He passed out. When doctors examined him, they said that he had been stabbed with some kind of 'thin tube'.

Just a few hours later, a second man was brought into the hospital – also with a strange wound on his neck. Exactly the same thing had happened to him, also in Coventry Street . . .

Unbelievably, a third patient later turned up at the same hospital. And guess what? He too had suffered a deep wound in his neck. The place? Coventry Street, of course.

The newspapers soon got hold of the strange story, and rumours began to spread that there was a dangerous vampire on the loose in the capital. Some said that the police had hired a vampire hunter, who was supposed to have chased the vampire and stabbed it through the heart. While no one knows if this is true, the attacks never happened again.

What do you make of this story? Could a real vampire have attacked the men in broad daylight? Did the victims themselves become vampires after they were attacked? These questions remain unanswered.

The Highgate Vampire

One of the spookiest places in London is a place called Highgate Cemetery. It is a large burial ground that dates back to Roman times, full of overgrown gravestones and scary-looking crypts.

Highgate Cemetery has always had a reputation for being haunted, but from the 1960s onwards, it was rumoured that a vampire stalked its ivy-strewn grounds . . .

Highgate Cemetery – wonder if there's a 'scaretaker' around?

It all started in 1963, when two schoolgirls taking a short cut through the cemetery reported seeing dead bodies rising from their tombs. A few weeks later, a terrified couple said they had seen a hideous face hovering behind some iron railings.

Later, someone said they had found the bodies of dead foxes – completely drained of blood – in the cemetery. Victims of thirsty vampires? It was rumoured that a member of the 'undead' had been brought to England from Wallachia (south of Transylvania) in a coffin during the eighteenth century and buried here. The legend of the Highgate Vampire was born.

More scary incidents occurred there over the years. A young woman described how she was attacked and thrown to the ground by a tall figure dressed in black with a deathly white face. The spooky man apparently vanished when a car stopped to help her.

The last recorded sighting was made in 2005 by a person returning to his home near Highgate Cemetery. A dark figure whispered to him as he passed the cemetery gates – 'Good evening, sir'! Not sure if the person hung around to reply . . .

Since then Highgate Cemetery has gone very quiet. Has the vampire gone elsewhere – or was there anything there in the first place?

Everything You Need to Know About Vampires

Is it obvious that someone is a vampire? Would you know for sure if you came across one in everyday life? Vampire hunters – here's a checklist of what to look out for:

- Vampires sleep in a coffin, or a grave, during the day
- They have very pale skin and pointed fang-like teeth

- Their lips are red (all that blood), and apparently their breath stinks. (Is that what's known as 'bat' breath?)
- Vampires can't bear sunlight – they can only go out in darkness, as light either burns or kills them
- They don't sleep or eat food – only blood will do
- A true vampire has no reflection when looking in a mirror and casts no shadow
- They have hypnotic powers and can use mind control with humans to get what they want
- Many have 'super-senses' giving them ultra-sensitive hearing, smell and vision
- Vampires are shapeshifters – they can change into other forms, mostly bats, wolves and also clouds of gas. That means they can get under cracks in doors and around windows . . . *eek*!

Vampires do differ slightly in different parts of the world: Russian vampires are supposed to have purple faces (should make them 'berry' easy to spot, then?). But one thing we're agreed on is that vampires everywhere are scary and it's best not to mess with them. Especially when they fancy a quick bite . . .

Where Do Vampires Come From?

When a person dies, many people believe that their 'soul' passes on into the next world. The 'next world' might be heaven, hell or some other form of afterlife, depending on your beliefs.

Vampires are said to be created when a person's soul can't pass on to the next world, and it is forced to stay inside the

body of the dead person. But why? Perhaps the person has done something wicked or has upset the Church in some way. Some cultures think that a vampire is created when a body isn't buried properly or because the Devil has taken over the body. They have even come up with some ways of preventing a dead body turning into a vampire – for instance:

- Nailing the corpse down inside the coffin – to stop it getting out in the night in search of blood
- Burying the body with lots of smelly garlic or 'holy bread' (bread which has been blessed by a priest)

Evidence of this kind of practice was recently unearthed in Bulgaria, when archaeologists found old skeletons with iron rods inserted through their chests – clearly done to prevent the bodies from becoming vampires. Or had the ghost of Vlad the Impaler been at work?

How to Get Rid of a Vampire

There's no doubt that having a vampire around can be a real pain in the neck! So how do you get rid of one that's breathing down yours? There are a few ideas about this. Some believe that a whiff of garlic usually sees them off, while others think more drastic measures are called for.

So should a Dracula-like figure turn up on your doorstep, the first rule is – *never ask them inside*. Vampires can only come into your house if they are invited. And once they're in, they can come back as many times as they want!

Here are a few other tips for getting rid of an unwanted bloodsucker:

- Expose it to sunlight – maybe keep the vampire talking till dawn so it's too late for it to get back to its coffin?

- Fill your house with garlic – vampires hate it! Garlic has long been prized for its pure, medicinal qualities and many believe that it can drive evil away
- Ward off the vampire with anything holy, such as a crucifix, holy water or an object that has been blessed by a priest. Some believe that vampires cannot walk over the ground of a church or temple either
- Find a mirror and hang it on the door – as you know, vampires don't have a reflection and they really don't like facing up to it!

- Get close to a stream or river – vampires apparently can't cross running water
- And finally – if all else fails – the ultimate solution is to find the grave or coffin of the vampire and hammer a wooden stake or dagger through its heart. (In some cultures, a suspected vampire corpse is burned and beheaded instead.) Obviously, you would need to do this during the day when the vampire is sleeping. And you would need to be pretty brave. Because there'd be a lot at 'stake' . . .

Bats and Blood

Whether or not you think vampires are real, there is one real-life creature that does a very good impression of one. It drinks blood, has sharp teeth, comes out at night – and it's called a vampire bat. Actually, in many movies and books, vampires take on the form of a bat at night – a very handy way for them to get around and into places to find victims.

The vampire bat lives mainly in Central and South America. Like all bats, it is nocturnal and emerges at dusk. It uses its own radar system, called 'echolocation', to move about and to find prey in the darkness. Talking of prey, in the case of the vampire bat, any warm-blooded mammal such as a cow – or a human – will do.

The vampire bat doesn't exactly have fangs but it does have very sharp front teeth, which it uses to make a tiny hole in the victim's skin. There is a special substance in the bat's saliva that prevents the blood from clotting so that it can keep drinking. As it operates at night, its victims are often sleeping when the attack happens – the person may not even realize they've been 'bloodsucked'. The bat meanwhile can drink up to half its body weight in blood! But if it can't get blood for two nights in a row, it will usually die.

You wouldn't want to 'hang around' with this 'bat' boy!

A Beastly Bat Bite

In the seventeenth century, Spanish explorers – 'Conquistadores' – journeyed to the Americas in search of gold and other glittering treasures. But they soon began to suffer from an unknown and terrifying sickness. Many of them died – and no one knew why. But over time, it dawned on the explorers that those who were getting ill also seemed to have small bite marks on their bodies. What was happening to them?

At night, the explorers slept in local caves, which seemed a good place to shelter. But the cause of the sickness was finally discovered when someone noticed that bats living in the caves were landing on the men at night – and biting them! In fact, what the vampire bats were actually doing (while they were drinking the men's blood) was passing on a fatal disease called rabies – but the Spaniards had no idea of this. They thought that the bats were draining them of their precious blood. Still, the men did stay out of the caves from then on, which helped prevent many more deaths.

In real life, vampire bats don't drain their victims of blood but, as the Conquistadores found out to their cost, they can pass on some very nasty diseases. They are best avoided!

MY MISSION

The only way I'll know for sure if vampires exist is to actually see one for myself. So my mission will happen at night, when vampires are supposed to come out in search of victims . . .

And, as vampires live in graves or coffins, the most obvious place to look for them would be a graveyard. Highgate Cemetery, once the home of a suspected vampire, sounds perfect, so that's where I'll start. I'll be sitting up all night with my camera (that shouldn't be difficult – could *you* manage to doze off in a graveyard?), ready to capture whatever emerges from the shadows.

The only drawback is – I'm scared. Really scared. It's going to be incredibly creepy in a graveyard at night on my own. Forget about vampires – what about ghosts – or even zombies? I'm not sure which is worse . . .

And if I do see a real vampire, the chances are that the vampire will be even more delighted to see me. A human victim ready and waiting – without having to travel!

I definitely need to protect myself. I've decided to dress completely in black to try and conceal myself in the darkness. Maybe then the vampire won't see me.

And I'll have an extensive supply of objects to ward off any Draculas who might feel like a drink.

KIT LIST

- NIGHT-VISION GOGGLES – these infrared stealth goggles attach to the head so that I can quite literally see in the dark (and have my hands free to ward off possible attacks)
- CAMERA WITH FLASH – mounted on a tripod (in case my hands are shaking!)
- DARK TROUSERS, JUMPER AND BALACLAVA (to blend in)
- HIGH-INTENSITY ALUMINIUM TORCH (for shining into those dark corners)
- COMFY CUSHION TO SIT ON (gravestones can be a bit hard and cold, I find)
- VERY THICK, VERY LONG SCARF – not because of the cold, but to wrap around my neck several times. Try and get your fangs through that, Dracula!

For protection

- As many bulbs of stinky garlic as I can carry – I'll hang a few around my neck as well, to be on the safe side
- Around my neck will also be a large crucifix; actually, several crucifixes – you can never be too careful . . .
- A hand mirror – I'll keep it in my pocket so I can get it out quickly if necessary and shove it in the vampire's face
- Most importantly – and this could be a lifesaver – a wooden stake and hammer: I've got a piece of old fencing from my garden and a mallet that I normally use for hammering tent pegs (I'm hoping these will do if things get serious)

MISSION COMPLETED

The night spent in the graveyard was indeed scary. And tiring. And dark. I didn't sleep a wink. At about four a.m., something caught my eye and I looked up to see a dark, cloaked shape moving across the corner of the graveyard. Then I heard harsh breathing close by – then felt cold breath upon my face! I clutched my garlic even harder and reached in my pocket for the mirror as a black shape loomed closer – then disappeared into the darkness. Was it a vampire – or just my imagination? I have no idea . . .

WHAT DO YOU THINK?

Vampires Don't Exist

While there are plenty of fictional vampires in movies, we've never actually caught a real one – alive or on film. Is this because they simply don't exist?

Many people think that this is the case – and that all the stories and legends about vampires stem from fear. Take a look at these two possible explanations for vampires.

1. Fear of Disease

Could the vampire myth be rooted in illnesses? In the past, when we didn't know much about medicine, many diseases seemed mysterious and frightening. People had no idea where diseases came from and how to treat them properly. Some illnesses – which we now know to be explainable and treatable – made victims appear or behave really strangely. And because people didn't understand why, they might have looked to vampires as a convenient explanation.

Take TB (tuberculosis), for example, a common disease in eighteenth- and nineteenth-century Europe. TB, if untreated, would make people very pale and thin over time. They would cough up blood and literally waste away – exactly what is supposed to happen if you become a vampire's victim (before you turn into one yourself). So it's likely that some victims of TB were believed to be victims of vampires.

Another 'vampire disease' is called *Erythropoietic Protoporphyria*. Try saying that with a pair of plastic fangs in your mouth . . . You'll be pleased to hear that this disease of the blood is incredibly rare. However, it was quite common among the rich families of Eastern Europe from the Middle Ages onwards. Which is exactly where many vampire legends circulated from.

Sufferers of this disease get reddish eyes, mouths and teeth. They become sensitive to sunlight, and if they go out in the light it can make their lips crack and bleed. Their lips also tighten and pull back from their mouths, so it looks like they're baring their teeth. As if all this didn't make them look vampire-ish enough, the poor victims were locked up during the day and let out at night.

So – what we've got is a bunch of desperately ill people – perhaps wearing dark cloaks – wandering about at night with red eyes and bared teeth. Well, you can see why people might have assumed that a bunch of vampires were on the prowl . . .

Another disease that can produce vampire-like symptoms is rabies, which is usually spread by animal bites. The Spanish explorers (see page 74) caught rabies from bats. Sufferers are sensitive to light and can become really aggressive. Symptoms can include making hoarse sounds, baring the teeth, frothing at the mouth and biting others.

It's interesting to note that vampire stories began circulating in Europe around the time that certain areas were experiencing

rabies. In Hungary between 1721 and 1728, for example, there was a terrible outbreak of rabies which killed dogs, wolves and humans. Not just a coincidence?

2. Fear of Death

People everywhere have always been fearful of death and of the 'dark side'. Some think that the vampire is an imaginary product of all these fears. If you think about it, having a fear of vampires was a useful thing for societies in the past. It made people stay faithful to the Church and encouraged them to lead good lives – so that there'd be less chance of them coming back as vampires after they'd died.

Another explanation related to death could be the strange behaviour of dead bodies. Corpses are creepy, no doubt. And they can sometimes do strange things. Muscles and tissue contract and tighten, which can make a corpse twitch suddenly and appear to move! Weird! It has even been reported that dead bodies can sometimes sit up suddenly on their own. This kind of thing was reported much more in the past, when dead bodies commonly used to be laid out in coffins in people's houses for days at a time, so that people could say their goodbyes.

One explanation for the movement is that gases in the stomach expand when the body decomposes. The stomach inflates like a balloon, which pulls the body upright. Whatever the explanation, if you were the person near the corpse you'd be pretty freaked out if it unexpectedly sat up! You could see why someone might think it was one of the 'living dead' – a vampire. Dead spooky!

Vampires Do Exist

This is going to be short. Because, as yet, there's no solid evidence that vampires are out there, stalking unwilling human victims at night. Sure, there are loads of stories, even eyewitness accounts, but no one has yet been on the news reporting sightings (or bitings) from a Dracula lookalike. There's only one night every year when vampires are guaranteed to be seen out and about – and that's Halloween!

Yet vampires have been around for so long, they are not going to go away, judging from the number of bestselling books and movies out there. Does this prove that there must be some truth in the vampire myth – or that humans are just fascinated by the idea of these chilling, bloodsucking creatures?

YOU DECIDE

So do you think vampires are mythical beings? Or that they are real? If it's the second option, I have one thing to ask you. Do you have a plan of action in case you are attacked by a vampire? If not, start thinking about it now . . . and perhaps note it down at the back so that you don't forget!

Werewolves

THE MISSION...

... is to find out if a human being can be transformed into a wolf...

> ## BURNING QUESTIONS
> 🔥 Are werewolves just monsters in horror movies?
> 🔥 Does the full moon have a magical effect?

MISSION DETAILS

You are alone in a dark forest. Through the branches you can see a full moon glowing in the night sky.

You hear a bloodcurdling howl behind you, and nervously turn to see – a gigantic, snarling wolf with fangs bared, about to pounce...

You are – a character in a werewolf movie! *Eek!*

A werewolf in a movie – probably made in 'Howlywood'!

Our mission is to find out more about werewolves – to really get inside their hairy skins. Could a person actually become a wolf in real life? Hunt down innocent people, then change back into a human with no memory of the terrible things they have done? Read on . . .

THE EVIDENCE

What is a werewolf? It looks like a much larger, scarier version of a real wolf. It has incredibly sharp fangs and can run incredibly fast. Victims have little chance against such a super-strong, powerful and vicious creature.

Werewolves are supposed to be humans who have undergone a weird shapeshifting process. The word itself comes from the Saxon word *wer* which means man – 'manwolf'.

If you've ever seen a human change into a werewolf in a movie, you'll know it's a terrifying transformation. As the moon shines down, the person screams in pain as their bones creak and extend painfully into the hulking form of a wolf. They stare down at their limbs in horror, as long brown hairs begin sprouting. Finally their face changes, becoming elongated and hairy, with pointed ears and yellow, staring eyes. They are 100 per cent werewolf and there's nothing they can do! Although, to be honest, I've never seen this end bit in a movie; I'm always behind the sofa by then.

This is no 'furry tale' ending

The werewolf goes out on a killing spree to satisfy its cravings. Unsurprisingly, it likes to 'wolf' down its food! But when dawn breaks, the werewolf returns to its normal, human form. It may or may not have any memory of the chaos it has caused during the night . . .

Changing Shape

Stories of 'shapeshifters' – creatures that can take the form of other animals – are found all around the world. Among them are:

- The Aswang of the Philippines – a creature that turns itself into a dog to eat human flesh
- The Kitsune of Japan – foxes that can turn into humans
- The Icelandic Hammrammr – can change into any animal that it has just eaten, getting more powerful each time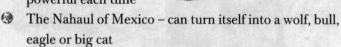
- The Nahaul of Mexico – can turn itself into a wolf, bull, eagle or big cat
- The Russian Wawkalak – surprisingly friendly werewolves, who lick hands instead of biting them!

But of all the shapeshifters around, the werewolf is the most well-known. Legends and stories go way back in time. In ancient Greece some doctors believed that people could change into wolves. The famous Greek historian Herodotus (480–425 BC) wrote about a tribe of people in north-eastern Europe called the Neuri who, he said, could change themselves into wolves once a year. In Greek myth, Zeus, the ruler of all the Greek gods, decided to punish King Lycaon by turning him into a wolf.

King Lycaon gets barking mad . . .

The legends persisted. In the Middle Ages, people had very strong beliefs in the power of witchcraft, magic and the Devil. It was commonly thought that those humans who were secretly werewolves had hair on the *inside* of their skin. The idea was that the person somehow turned themselves 'inside out' when they changed into a wolf! People could quite easily be accused of being a werewolf and sent to trial. It might sound silly to us now, but a few hundred years ago, it was nothing to laugh about. Mainly because the only way to find out for sure if someone was a secret werewolf was to cut open the person to see if they were hairy on the inside! That's a 'furry' bad result for the suspect!

Those people thought to be werewolves often endured horrible fates. In France in the sixteenth and seventeenth centuries, thousands of people were sent to trial, tortured and burned at the stake. Many were innocent of any wrongdoing – though some did admit to committing crimes as 'wolves'.

Wolves or Men?

In 1521 two men called Burgot and Verdum were sent to their deaths after they confessed to rubbing themselves with 'magic ointment' (see page 193), turning into hairy wolves and killing several people. In another incident, in 1603, a man named Jean Grenier admitted that he had killed several people while in the shape of a wolf. He had a special wolfskin that apparently turned him into a beast.

Similarly, in Germany, a man called Peter Stubbe was executed

in 1589 when he was found guilty of killing hundreds of people. He also said that he had turned himself into a wolf by putting on a wolfskin belt.

Was there any truth in all this shapeshifting – or was it just an excuse for murder? These cases happened so long ago we will probably never know.

But can belts and skins turn people into wolves? Some legends say so – and there are many other reasons why you might accidentally become a werewolf. To help you avoid them, I have compiled a handy checklist.

How to become a werewolf:

- Have you been bitten by any furry, ferocious beasts recently? According to just about every book, movie and TV programme made on the subject, the most common way of becoming a werewolf is to get bitten by one
- Have you ever slept outdoors under a full moon?
- Were you born on a Friday when there was a full moon?
- Have you ever drunk water from a footprint made by a wolf?
- Are you the youngest of seven children?
- Do you ever wear a skin or a belt made of wolfskin?
- Do you ever rub magic ointment onto your body? These special ointments are thought to contain magical plants like belladonna and henbane
- Have you ever been cursed?

If any of the above sound familiar, then watch out (or perhaps your family and friends should)!

The Beast of Gévaudan

A well-known story from France describes how, in 1764, about 40 people were savagely killed and more than 100 injured by an unknown wild creature, or creatures. The attacks happened over several years in the mountainous province of Gévaudan. Those who saw the beast said it was a reddish wolf-like creature, as large as a cow and a very fast runner.

A woman tries to fight back against the beast.

Three years after the first attack, a massive wolf was found and shot by a hunter, using a silver bullet. The wolf's body was paraded through the village, but rumours flew around that the beast was *not* actually the real killer. People thought that the guilty creature had been hidden by the authorities – because it had turned back into its human form, and they didn't want anyone to know who it was! Meanwhile, the attacks stopped and the people of Gévaudan could breathe easily again. Today a statue remembering the beast's victims still stands in the town but the mystery remains, well, a mystery.

Fewer werewolf sightings seem to be reported these days. However, a couple more modern stories might give you something to think about . . .

The Bray Road Beast

In the quiet countryside of Wisconsin, USA, several sightings of a large hairy wolf-like creature walking on its hind legs were reported in the late 1980s. According to those who saw it, the 'Beast' had long claws, yellow eyes and a terrifying stare. It was rather whiffy too – whenever it was spotted there seemed to be a nasty smell around! One witness – a young lady who saw it loping down the road – said it was a 'very powerful, fast runner'. And as yet no one has identified the mystery monster . . .

The Morbach Monster

Stories say that the town of Wittlich in Germany is haunted by a werewolf, who is supposed to be the ghost of a soldier from the time of Napoleon. He deserted the army and killed a farmer and his wife. Before she died, the wife cursed the soldier

and now, at every full moon, he becomes a werewolf. But the villagers keep a shrine and a candle lit just outside the town to protect them. Legend has it that if the candle ever goes out, the werewolf will return . . .

In 1988 a group of men working for the US military were on the way to their jobs at Morbach (an air force base just outside the town) when they noticed that the candle had gone out. They all joked about the monster then went about their work.

Late that night, an alarm went off at the perimeter fence of the base and the men went to investigate. One of them said he saw a huge 'dog-like' animal stand up on its back legs, stare at him, and then jump directly over the two-metre-high fence. A military tracker dog was brought to the fence and found the creature's scent – but the dog absolutely refused to follow it. Was it fear of the werewolf that stopped him?

Full Moon Madness

Every werewolf story begins with a full moon. So what's so mysterious about the moon?

© BRIAN E. KUSHNER, GETTY IMAGES

The Moon: big, bright – and bewitching

A full moon has long been connected with changes in behaviour – even madness. In the past, people suffering from mental illness were said to behave strangely, even violently, when the moon came into its full phase. This gave us the word 'lunatic', which comes from 'lunar' – to do with the moon. (A more recent theory is that the patients behaved strangely because they were exhausted – the moon was so bright when it was full, that they simply couldn't get to sleep!)

Scientists know that something called gravitational pull exists between the Earth and the Moon. This force influences large bodies of water, particularly the movement of the tides on Earth.

Some people believe that gravitational pull must have a similar effect on humans. They think that because our bodies and brains are 80 per cent water, the Moon could influence our behaviour – especially when it is full. There is no scientific proof for this theory – but that doesn't stop lots of people believing it.

MY MISSION

To find a real werewolf! But where? Maybe I should go to places where there are still wolves roaming wild. Many wolf populations have died out over the years but in some parts of the world like the forests of Alaska and the Arctic tundra, wolves do still live in the wild. But what would I do if I found one? I'd better work out how to deal with it . . .

How to Get Rid of a Werewolf

After extensive research, I have compiled this handy – and hopefully foolproof – guide. If you ever find yourself up against a werewolf, do one of the following:

- Stab the wolf three times in the head with a knife
- Kneel in one spot for a hundred years (er – wouldn't you both be dead by then? I suppose that's one way of getting rid of a werewolf!)
- Find a wolfsbane plant. The only problem is that humans can't touch it – it is deadly poisonous to us. But it is hated by werewolves and is thought to act as a kind of 'wolf repellent'. Some think wolfsbane can even kill a werewolf
- Throw something made of iron at the wolf
- Some say that you need to get three drops of the wolf's blood. When the blood falls on the ground, the wolf should turn straight back into a human
- And last of all, the best-known and most effective solution – shoot it with a silver bullet. This should definitely rid you of a troublesome wolf

Wolfsbane – deadly to wolves and humans.

KIT LIST

I know exactly what I need to get – but buying these items from my local shops is proving tricky. There's not a silver bullet to be found anywhere. The local garden centre doesn't sell wolfsbane – and I can't touch it anyway. I'm not keen on doing 100 years of kneeling (even with knee pads on) and it's too dangerous to carry a knife. Werewolf hunters in movies don't seem to have this problem . . .

So what am I left with? Something made of iron . . . let me think. How about:

An Iron!

Maybe a household iron – as in, the thing you use to get creases out of clothes – would work!

It's all I've got, quite frankly, which is why I'm lugging a rather heavy carrier bag containing my iron (plus lead and plug). If nothing else, it will certainly make quite a dent in the werewolf's head if I throw it really hard . . .

MISSION COMPLETED

Silly me – I didn't need to go all the way to the Arctic tundra to find a wolf. I simply did the obvious thing – waited for the next full moon. Then it was time to go out on my werewolf hunt, iron at the ready.

At one point while walking nervously along a dark road, I heard a low, growling noise coming from round the corner. Then I saw a shadow looming – a shadow of a hairy beast! I got ready with my iron. Then round the corner came . . . a man walking a large shaggy dog. At that point I gave up and went home. Where's a werewolf when you need one? Perhaps they're all on 'howliday'?

WHAT DO YOU THINK?

Hopefully, by now you will have ruled out the possibility that you are a werewolf (I certainly have) and can turn your mind to the big question. Have werewolves ever existed?

Werewolves Don't Exist

There are several possible explanations for wolf myths – which one do you think is the most likely?

1. Fear of Animals

If you don't believe that werewolves exist, that's fair enough. But why are there so many stories about them? Where did they come from, if not from reality?

Some people think that that the whole werewolf myth springs from fear. Hundreds of years ago, wolves were much more of a threat to people than they are now. Imagine if you were living in a small village near a forest. You (and any livestock you owned) would be under constant threat of attack by roaming packs of hungry wolves. Wolves would have been a hot topic of conversation, creatures to be feared and dreaded.

And it's not just wolves. It's interesting that shapeshifting stories of humans turning into animals such as tigers, bears and foxes seem to exist in every culture. Is this because they are all about the real threat of local animals in times past?

Another theory is that people (deep down, maybe without even realizing it themselves) wish for the power that a particular animal has and want to experience it – hence their desire to change into a powerful tiger or a running wolf or a soaring eagle in flight. Who wouldn't want those kinds of powers?

Could human fears and wishes be at the root of all these

fantastic stories? Let's face it, they are great stories – which is why we're still telling them now!

2. Sickness and Disease

Just as with vampires, some think that the idea of werewolves has grown out of hideous diseases that have affected people over the centuries. The most obvious 'wolf sickness' is called lycanthropy. This is a weird one.

Lycanthropy is a mental illness in which a person believes that he/she has actually turned into a wolf (though they haven't actually grown any fur or sprouted big teeth). The disease was first noted in the seventh century, when victims were seen running about on four legs, barking and howling . . . literally 'barking mad'! It could certainly explain many of the past strange cases of people believing they have changed into wolves and killed people.

Another disease that could make people behave like a wolf is rabies, a virus which attacks the brain and nervous system and which could also be an explanation for vampire-like behaviour (see page 79). The disease makes people very feverish and aggressive and they can behave like crazed wild animals. They don't, however, grow fur . . . unlike the final 'wolf sickness' (also the strangest) – a rare condition called hypertrichosis.

Sufferers of hypertrichosis grow hair pretty much everywhere, even all over their face and hands. This can make someone look like a living wolf-man! In fact, years ago, the victims of this hair-raising condition were often forced to

make a living by becoming part of a freak show, for people to gasp and stare at (once they'd paid their money, of course).

A wolf-like appearance — but just the results of a rare condition

Could the idea of werewolves have come from seeing people who had some of these conditions?

3. Wolf Poison

In Europe, during the Middle Ages, it's fair to say that health and safety wasn't what it is today. You could travel in an open cart without a seatbelt on (gasp!), no one picked up their animals' poo or even cared about the state of playground equipment (probably because there wasn't any at that time).

There were, however, outbreaks of food poisoning. Some of the more serious cases were caused by a fungus called ergot, which grew on a grain called rye. Rye was used to make bread and the people who ate the infected bread were poisoned. The disease – called St Anthony's Fire because of the awful burning sensation it produced – badly affected the brain. Symptoms included grunting, shaking and violent behaviour. It also caused terrible hallucinations which made some of the victims think that they were turning into an animal!

Bread poisoning was quite widespread, affecting whole towns and communities – could its victims have been mistaken for werewolves?

Werewolves Do Exist

So – what is the evidence for the existence of werewolves? There isn't really any. We have no film of a real person changing

into a wolf. We have no photographs. And the last time I looked, there weren't a whole lot of werewolves on the loose being reported on in the news.

What we do have, though, are many fantastic stories, myths and legends – plus some very entertaining movies and TV shows. So, if you're the kind of person who believes that myths and legends really do have an element of truth in them, perhaps you do believe that werewolves exist? Or maybe you've actually seen a 'furry fiend' with your own eyes? If so, we need to know about it!

If you're a werewolf believer, you'll probably be keeping an eye out for anyone you know showing signs of 'werewolfness'. According to legend, these signs could be: extremely hairy hands, eyebrows that meet in the middle, hair on the palms of the hands or even hair in the ears. (So probably the best way of protecting yourself is to spend a lot of time with bald people . . .)

YOU DECIDE

So are werewolves a lot of nonsense, or do you shiver and shake on the night of a full moon? Only *you* can decide what you think is the truth about werewolves.

To the back of the book you go!

WANT TO KNOW MORE?

If you want to find out more about some of these intriguing creatures, try these books and websites:

Graphic Mysteries: Bigfoot and other strange beasts – Rob Shone (Book House)

You can't scare me! A guide to the strange and supernatural (Tick Tock Entertainment)

The Vampire Book – Sally Regan (Dorling Kindersley)

Can Science Solve? The Mystery of Vampires and Werewolves – Chris Oxlade (Heinemann)

Beastly Tales: Yeti, Bigfoot and the Loch Ness Monster – Malcolm Yorke (Dorling Kindersley)

My Quest for the Yeti: Confronting the Himalayas' deepest mystery – Reinhold Messner (Pan Macmillan)

www.nessie.co.uk – Lots of information about the Loch Ness monster, including latest sightings, evidence, stories and news

www.nationalgeographic.com – Great for all kinds of information about the world. You can search the site for their view on the creatures in this book

DECISION TIME

So, we've looked at the evidence (which sometimes got a bit too close for comfort, if you ask me). Now it's time for you to sort the facts from the fiction and solve some of the world's greatest mysteries once and for all . . .

Mystery 1: The Loch Ness Monster

Notes:

_____

_____

_____

Possible explanations:

☐ *1. Nessie Is a Plesiosaur*

☐ *2. Nessie Is a Giant Eel*

☐ *3. Nessie the Elephant?*

☐ *4. Nessie Is Tree Gas!*

☐ *5. Weird Waves*

☐ *6. Other* _____

Mystery 2: The Yeti

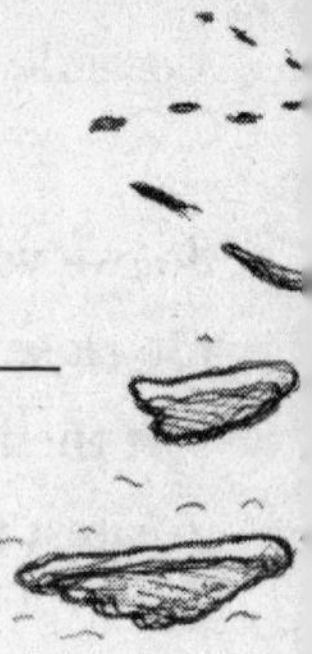

Notes:

_____

_____

_____

_____

Possible explanations:

☐ *1. The Yeti Doesn't Exist*

☐ *2. A Trick of the Sun?*

☐ *3. The Yeti Exists: It's a Giant Ape*

☐ *4. The Yeti Exists: It's a Man (Sort of . . .)*

☐ *5. Other* _____

Mystery 3: Vampires

Notes:

_____

_____

_____

_____

Possible explanations:

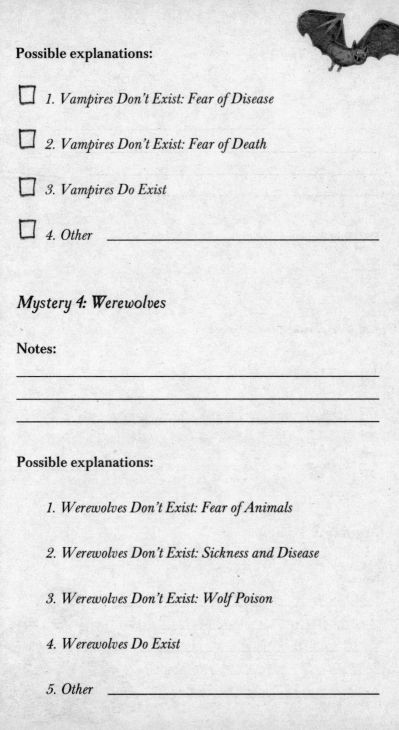

- [ ] *1. Vampires Don't Exist: Fear of Disease*

- [ ] *2. Vampires Don't Exist: Fear of Death*

- [ ] *3. Vampires Do Exist*

- [ ] *4. Other* _____

Mystery 4: Werewolves

Notes:

_____

_____

_____

Possible explanations:

1. *Werewolves Don't Exist: Fear of Animals*

2. *Werewolves Don't Exist: Sickness and Disease*

3. *Werewolves Don't Exist: Wolf Poison*

4. *Werewolves Do Exist*

5. *Other* _____

If you enjoyed this book, why not try
the other titles in the series?

GREAT MYSTERIES OF THE WORLD

ALIEN ENCOUNTERS
ANCIENT TREASURES
WEIRD WATERS

Read every out-of-this-world adventure!

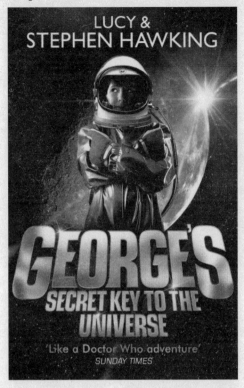

Take a ride through space and discover the
mysteries of science and the universe with
George and a super-intelligent computer
called Cosmos.

But someone else would like to get their hands
on Cosmos – someone whose power-hungry
plans will lead George to a black hole and
sure-fire deep space danger.

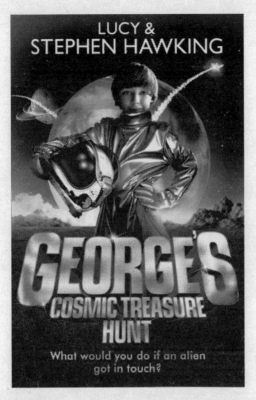

LUCY &
STEPHEN HAWKING

GEORGE'S
COSMIC TREASURE
HUNT

What would you do if an alien
got in touch?

George's best friend Annie needs help.
She has discovered something really weird
on her dad's super-computer.

Is it a message from an alien? Could there be
life out there? And if you could talk to aliens,
what would you say?

Join George as he battles a sinister rebel-scientist,
who's hell bent on sabotaging the most exciting –
and dangerous – experiment of the century.

A deadly bomb is ticking.
The whole world is watching.
Can George stop the second big bang?

**Meet Itch – an accidental, accident-prone hero.
Science is his weapon. Elements are his gadgets.**

Richard Hammond invites you to journey with him to the planet's most puzzling places . . .

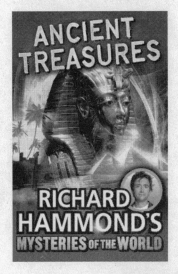

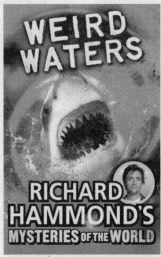

Can you solve the mystery?